André Sneed

YOUR PERSPECTIVE IS NOT MY REALITY

I0558630

Also by André Sneed

"The Ideology of my Imagination"

André Sneed

Your Perspective Is Not My Reality

by

André Sneed

Dedication

To all my children, grandchildren, extended family, friends, fans, and followers.

To all those who strive daily and who are fueled by perseverance and a passion for greatness. Continue to be unapologetically different, living your own truth regardless of other's perspective of normal.

André Sneed

Your Perspective is Not My Reality

Published by André Sneed. Cover design by Limit Creative Agency. Printed in the United States of America Publisher's Cataloging-in-Publication data

ISBN 9798218249311

Library of Congress Control Number TXu 2-366-777

Developmental editing by Legacy Book Coaching & Consulting

André Sneed

Table of Contents

André Sneed

FOREVER

If I take a plane and fly away
Landing at Paradises pearly gate
I'd have no regrets today or yesterday
Making way for you to take the place.

At the top of our mighty lineage
It's rather thick, tall and strong
Your foundation is a sturdy pyramid
Make a decision, trust it, and push on.

Lead the pack and rarely follow
May your yesterdays pave your tomorrows
If you want it, go get it at all costs
Don't limit yourself and rarely borrow.

Be aware of your surroundings
The streets never sleep but they teach
Hustle hard because everything earned
Is sweet like vacations on a sandy beach.

Bills are forever but know your worth
Never forget to pay yourself first
Eat now and drink your cocktails later
And never allow the trap of sneaky thirst.

You are God's child and then mine
So never dance to the beat of another drum
The only set of fingerprints, one of a kind
You were made unique you equal one!

I can go on about how to move
But many lessons I have already instructed
Some lessons you have to gain in time
But trust the blueprint previously constructed.

Do not waste your time, it is the currency of life
The only thing you can't get back
So take what you need for this trip
Anything weighing heavy, leave that.

Always compare you to yourself
Measure success in the mirror
If you see love, health, and wealth
Then, life's vision will become clearer.

I love you always and you know it
Always remain fearless and the boldest
This is just a letter to all my beloved
From the youngest seed to my oldest.

Dedicated to my queens and my king
Place it in your soul, and know this
In regards to the matters of my heart
Forever is the duration that you own it.

QUESTIONS

Stop asking the wrong questions
You're dating, and that's cool
But while they are spitting game
Ask more than where did you go to school.

What are your interests?
What do you like in a partner?
Ask them where they see themselves
In five years, for starters.

What is their credit score?
What is their relationship with God?
Do they want a family?
I mean real content before the nod.

Protect your future, be aware
Talking, no this is an interview
Don't waste each other's time
Want a key, first get a clue.

You don't need a boo
Rather, try to obtain a partner in life
Sex is straight, but a little taste
Won't aid your dreams at night.

That life you live during the day
Balancing work and play
Watch how they keep their house
Who else lives where they stay?

How do they get their pay?
Are they stuck in their ways?
Or open to change, somewhat strange

While walking, does their gaze go astray?

Will they support your dreams?
Play a part on the team?
Share your vision on life, cook,
What's their definition of clean?

Be specific on things
Will they want you to change?
More than self-betterment
But more like for personal gain?

We all have skeletons
But do they have damaging stains?
Have they healed from their childhood?
Or will they cause a relationship strain?

Question yourself
What are you willing to resist
Know your wills and will nots
Have you made your list?

If you do this off top
You will save some time
And if you think it's too soon
Please go back about two lines.

What is their take on stock
Generational wealth or being rich
Do they own or want to own property
Or permanently fixed in their niche?

Do they like to travel
What do they constantly aspire
Are they happy being a worker bee
Or an entrepreneur doing the hiring?

Questions, it's the questions you ask
That makes a difference
If you don't ask the right questions
You're stuck in their representative's mission.

SHADOWBOXING II

Two to the chin
What makes you think you can win
Back into the lion's den
Oh! You thought you had a friend?

Need to do a better job of fending
For yourself right now and again
Don't get yourself done in
I hate a coward that pretends.

Overhand left with a grin
Don't wrap up, spend
Time is money, I got ends
Heavyweight gloves on my pen.

Watching my back like a fin
Execution is my next of kin
So your chances here are slim
Won't measure up to my limbs.

Fired an upper on a whim
Caught your eye, camera lens
Trying to lock me up like the pen
Get hit when my knuckles bend.

Blows to the midsection
I fall victim to misdirection
Deviated from the lesson
Got away from my training session.

Not at all what I was expecting
The enemy has me guessing
Without a word, I left my weapon
Searching for a resurrection.

André Sneed

Once again it's only me in the fight
Shadowboxing for dear life
In desperate need to fly a kite
Walking quickly into the light.

Doing away with the anxious
Planting my roots among the tainted
Showing proof is rather ageless
Look within and make the changes.

HUES

Idealists see black and white
Realists recognize the Gray
People with tunnel vision lack depth
Give me vision with lots of shade.

The everyday aura of green
See the love and balance in life
Enjoying family and nature
The integrity to do what is right.

You can see the inner peace
Our inner child keeps us mellow
A confident and passionate
Spirit animal draped in yellow.

Give me fields of orange
Like the warmth from the sun
With positivity uplifting
Possessing a joy second to none.

Studying others' patterns and dialogue
So you will know how to move
A chameleon of sorts
But communicating in blue.

Hopefully not confused
With the non-dissipated flow
Energy will continue to transfer
In its truest shade of indigo.

The vision of the now
Never letting moments sink

André Sneed

Living in the here and now
What a radiant shade of pink.

I love the intuitive
Maximized greatness of hurdles
The dreamer, artist, poet
The undeniable royal purple.

To the love of goals and passion
A hunger that must be well fed
Relating to whole-body intimacy
Is left for the color of red.

Silver is for the blessings
Glowing in great abundance
Shining down from the head
Wow, that armor is something.

What about the beam
That is dominant and bold
A gleam that will not tarnish
A respectful nod to the gold.

We know what the darkness
And the basic foundation brings
But a prism breeds a rainbow
Hues in life's color scheme.

HIGH & WAVE

Chasing my first high for decades
Forget chemically engineered drugs
Not flowers, alcohol or playing spades
Never fallen short in the area of love.

You may never even understand
What pumps the heart of a man
That strives not from testosterone
But the hormone from the adrenaline gland.

Imagine a rush that drives your body
To process your fears into fuel
Fight or flight, we are never scared
Blessed with an internal mechanism tool.

On that Friday after school
The first party I attended as a freshman
I was holding up the wall
But shortly after, I learned a life lesson.

The music took over me
I shed my fears of crowds and image
I walked to the middle of the dance floor
A far cry from being timid.

I hopped and hollered out my block
And as a matter of fact
Bouncing, dancing, and standing proud
The entire party joined the act.

I knew at this moment
I was born to live the party life
But what I didn't know at this moment

André Sneed

This would be my ultimate high.

Doing many things strange
For so long, minus the change
But the tales I will not express or name
Just out of respect for the estranged.

They may call me insane
Crazy, wild, down, nuts or game
Some things they will never call me
Is tamed, fake, lame or plain.

For those of you around
While I've been chasing this trip
You're welcome, and did you die
No, so actually you owe me a tip.

And if I rise on this day
And God picked up the cards I laid
There is not anything that I would change
Especially not that first high and wave.

TRUE NORTH

My life revolves like an exercised mouse
From the slow lane to the median
Quicker than my ride on 271 South
Spinning out of control, speeding.

Watching the cars slow down
In the middle of my forged 360s
Praying to God for safety
During the thick of rush hour, no one hit me.

So miss me, with the talk
Of the damaged moral compass
Even with a protractor
You couldn't match my circumference.

Don't lump us, but I want you to win
But tend to pass judgment on the next
Climb up out the ditch that we're all in
We're a work in progress, He isn't done yet.

Unless, you give up on yourself
Throwing in the hand you were naturally dealt
Is it the wealth that has you moving stealth
Rid the red from your ledger, focus on health.

Tighten your belt, and diminish waves
Straight lines are looking more appeasing these days
It's your face you view everyday
Do you see joy or one who needs to be saved?

Who am I, one who I believe in
Full of love and integrity, a real friend

André Sneed

Time and again, people run their mouth
But beware of individuals directing you south.

Misdirection is common in warfare
Is this thing on, is there anyone out there
Blank stares as if vision is impaired
If you're about positivity, many won't care.

Shock value has their attention these days
Some see the maze, some seem to be amazed
Listen close and take heed of the course
Keep your head on a swivel; always travel true north.

DEFINITION OF A MAN

He will be concerned about your status
And what you will grow to be
Placing effort in your cause
Without your vision being seen.

Telling you that you are gifted
And can succeed in whatever you want
You can be wealthy, but the streets watch
So be careful not to flaunt.

Teaching lessons about the world
And how things work
Somewhat different from a mother
Who doesn't want you to get hurt.

Reality is hard but fair
So prepare for the haul
Leaving instructions in the mind
Helping to prevent a fall.

Yet he emphasizes you will fall
But don't fall the same twice
Place value on life and of course
You will have to sacrifice.

Telling you to trust in your faith
And do not forget to pray
All your goals may be reached
By conquering obstacles in your way.

Saying to respect yourself and others
And demand respect too
If you are unsure in a situation

André Sneed

Place your foot in another's shoe.

When your thoughts feel like fantasy
He will say they are the best scenes
His knowledge breeds wisdom
He supports all of your dreams.

He will tell you not to cry
Worry, or submit to temper
Invest in changing all your situations
All without a whimper.

We all need a little help
But to support your own way
So please support this message
Every day is Father's Day.

He is God fearing, child-rearing
A protector of values
Genuinely loving, placing others first
With a positive attitude.

He is driven, ambitious
A leader by design
Cultivator, a mind stimulator
A master of configured time.

He is giving, an active listener
Always constructing a plan
A double helix of greatness
The definition of a man.

MY DAWGS

A mans best friend is a dawg
A being by his side to see him through it all
To bark at the haters and bite in a brawl
Supporting his man, not letting him fall.

Your dawg is family and walks the same way
Your dawg is by your side no matter where you stay
You never want to get caught sleeping, yet sometimes you do
Your dawg will be your guard, letting you know what to do.

A man with personality and a few flaws
Is in need of true company like a few dawgs
No tears or pain, for dawgs help you feel
Best believe the big dawgs are known to keep it real.

Dedicated to the dawgs, the men on our right
By our side during every important day in this life
The ones a part of a pack, pact with brotherly love
An unbreakable bond fueled by the spirits above.

Bark a role call and pump your fists in the air
Shout out to the other one percenter's out there
Keeping your eyes open and speaking without vowels
I know the dawgs are on point when I hear the growls.

ANXIETY

I hear it coming, I hear it coming
A message to my mind from my heart
You feel that, a sharp piercing
The silent killer, shooting deadly darts.

Is it a wave, a paraphrase
Metaphors of demons that impair
A simple feeling or a thought
May trigger the luring presence in the air.

It can cripple you if you allow
We think we need a substance to rid
The sleepless nights, exhaustion gripes
A maze of thoughts, not wanting out of bed.

Is it just me, why can't I breathe
My heart's pounding, I'm awake, I think
Foggy days like tidal waves
I'm on the ledge, better yet the brink.

Feeling like a kink
A widespread restriction of being free
No handicap, yet an issue
A private or social unease.

Panic attacks, rough idle breathing
Sneaking through the veins
When are you leaving
God don't let my belief prove as vain.

I trust you, I need you now
More than ever, my temple is flawed

A story with many tiny deaths a day
Picture the ending, no round of applause.

André Sneed

EUPHORIA*

When you first catch the word
That tickets are going on sale
The excitement fills you slightly
And you do more than inhale.

Gasping with shock
And now starts the plan
I have to solidify my presence
Must have my feet in the stands.

I cop the tickets
Now I have to figure out my fit
I must represent the artist
My concert tee must be lit.

Now I need a playlist
With all my artists' favorite hits
Rekindling memories with the music
Remember this, that's my ish!

Now it's a vibe
Tracks on repeat in my ride
I need to explore the lyrics
Ensure the words are fresh in my mind.

Preparing for the moments
All throughout the night
When the emcee moves the crowd
Inciting participation with the mic.

All of this feels right
I smile, I laugh, I dance, I sing

I rap, I love, I live
I'm enjoying absolutely everything.

The music makes me high
Maybe even the aroma in the sky
The beat, the hook, the mood
All the goers present, one common tie.

The official apparel after the show
The signature from the artist
Ears ringing from the loud speakers
Now, reminiscing on the show gets started.

Once we leave the doors of the venue
What's on the menu
With an empty stomach and a full spirit
I love what I got into.

Definitely worth the price of admission
Storing my tickets for keepsake
Something about the euphoria of music
Like an addict chasing that first taste.

*Featured on the music track All lies by N.O.M.A.D (on all streaming platforms)

André Sneed

SOCIOPATHS

It's a lifetime prison sentence
The second they stole our innocence
Walking around with bald fists
The world wondering why we're so tense.

What's on your credit card
A piece of it resides on my shoulder
We thought it would dissipate
Just as soon as we got a little older.

But all we got is a little colder
Found out how to be a true soldier
Live life in the now and be stronger
Shrink our mountains to small boulders.

Raise our valleys to the skyline
And ultimately flunk you if you test mine
And the magic is bold like an outline
Live in Seattle rain, yet we still shine.

Who am I, I'm my circumstances
On the contrary, I'm here for a lesson
It's like showing up to the wrong class
But raising your hand that you're present.

Nothing worse than a grown man cry
Cowards hate the truth, so won't look in my eye
If I can be anything, you ask
Give me some wings so I can fly.

So I no longer have to chase a high
To grow opportunities and bury trauma
Letting go of absolutely everything

Dreadful, before the "But God" comma.

Undercompensated and underprivileged
But you can't blame that on my village
With the exact same qualifications
We're overlooked, once again pillaged.

Continually striving for excellence
No matter if we finish first or last
Our environment incites anger
The wrath of a sociopath.

André Sneed

THE CONUNDRUM

How is it that people actually see
On local and national tv
Certain people get killed by the police
But turn their nose up looking at me.

When I believe in the conspiracy
And they define insanity
As the same thing happens frequently
An outcome of a repetitive plea.

When things do not make sense
They still continue to believe
But will quickly frown their face
When I say that Jesus freed me?

How can one not think
On a level of conscious and free
They say they aren't slaves
But if we could ask technology.

Ever wonder why some things
Come without a price
Won't let social media mediate me
But staying connected sounds nice.

Protect your body and your mental
Why is organic so special
Processed food is killing us daily
Without guns, so it's considered gravy.

But don't get it confused
We still are being used
Secure your persons and where you stay

Pushed agenda by the rifle between NA.

But population control is not a thing
It only happens in dictatorship
But explain how we lost our privacy
With more items adding to the list.

Like what we place in our temple
They name it instrumental
A new constitute of the constitution
Secret Society deems essential.

How quickly they forget the manifesto
After the inauguration commenced
Is it a strain on your brain believing
Capitalism is governed by the one percent?

I'm just scratching the surface
Hoping I can reach someone
Wondering whose third eye is open
And there lies the conundrum.

André Sneed

INTRODUCTIONS

It started in my toddler days
I remember as early as the second page
In my book of life, before all the rage
Introduced to death, yet I stayed.

I remember having a best friend
At just the age of ten
He hit me in the head with a brick
My introduction to games you can't win.

Around the same time
I was being consoled after dark
I remember a parallel reality
Sexually, too young at its start.

Which in hindsight, brought upon
My introduction to flowers and alcohol
I remember doing everything
At twelve, except, walking around the mall.

Honestly, I remember doing much
In life way too soon
Like my introduction to therapy
Sharing my feelings in a room.

Confiding in my friends
I considered them more like brothers
Yet, I remember being pressured into a set
My introduction to colors.

In high school, I was underweight
But I was introduced to scales

I remember, yet another beginning
The start of my addiction to sales.

Ahead of the curve being distant
At the top, you get blatant
I remember being parent free
My introduction to an unofficial emancipation.

By college, I'd done it all
These kids were late to the no good
I remember my next phase
The introduction to fatherhood.

Precocious and I remember it all
The years of an internal fight
Thankful for what saved my life
My introduction to Christ.

André Sneed

PRECOCIOUS MEMORIES

I'm really overwhelmed with what's happening
She smiled while we ate
I know what's coming
But why, I'm only eight?

As she washed the plate
I dried the cups
She peeked, ensuring no one is looking
Then she touched my butt.

Enough is enough
I feel weird during these interactions
Too young to make decisions
And was told its okay, when asking.

To her satisfaction
She made me half of the team
I suppressed the memories
But cunnilingus set spark at fourteen.

I remember this taste
Removing a smile from my face
But the fellas on my block
Told me tail I should chase.

So I save face
And began my second chapter
Depression would set after
Yet, I became quite the actor.

So as the years led me
I used sex as a coping mode

This is the way I showed my love
It is the only way I know.

My greatest gift, I thought
And my greatest enemy
Maybe the reason some are free
You would call my kind a freak.

One who never met his peak
A playboy in the sheets
Practice made me imperfect
Never satisfied emotionally.

The third chapter brought control
Or so I thought
But knowledge of self was once revealed
When all was lost.

I practiced abstinence for months
Gained control of my urges
Let the walls down and healed
Minimizing the surges.

I am thankful for vision
God's plan and submission
Sex is more than a weapon
For some, it is an addiction.

André Sneed

P.T.S.D.

She awoke to screams in another room
He was curled up in a ball
Sweating and feeling like being in a tomb
She looked into his eyes and saw a wall.

She desperately attempted to wake him
Visions impaired, he didn't see her at all
Trying to unclench his fist prior to the sin
Like a bad dream, worse than the fall.

He was stuck in a mental maze
He had a gun, oh the pain he was in
Reliving the memory, the brick paved
So much blood, sweat and tears once again.

He was nude and erratic; his body was cold
His temper was hot, he is out of control
One would think this is his only mental break
But unfortunately, the last is merely a goal.

He'd seen so much good in this life
But the bad weighed really heavy
Don't ask him how he's doing
For his answer, trust you are not ready.

It feels like evil broke the levee
And his cranium is flooding itself
If the mind is our motherboard
His operating system has outdated his health.

But the man is not alone in the sequence
Many are suffering from frequent defeat

Entrapped by the depths of our mind
Yet granted furlough to walk the streets.

Whether it be abandonment issues
Resulting to being cold at heart
When they finally let you in
Leaving unannounced, will create a spark.

A glimpse into an emotion
A past wound that can always reopen
The highest form of loneliness
Filled with alcohol and smoking.

It may be sexual perversions
Maybe even more like an assault
What should be so kind and special
Ends in an innocence lost.

Now there is an absence of love
Detect side eye vision in our optometry
Hugs and touches are unwanted
A confusion of pure intimacy.

Our exterior may look normal and neat
We could be clean from head to feet
But you never know what someone goes through
So be mindful and beware of P.T.S.D.

André Sneed

RELEASE

Tear dropped pillows, weeping like willows
The pain is unbearable
I am broken and my emotions
And demeanor are hysterical.

I cannot control myself
I miss my soul
Death to romance flicks and love songs
I'm bawling like I'm five years old.

I cannot fight the grief
My anxiety is evolving
I believe in God and His love
But right now, my toxicity is the problem.

How can I make it right?
Do my kids hate me too?
I once was the king of this palace
Now I just feel like the royal fool.

God help me, I need you now
Right now, in fact
I don't care what people think
I'll do anything to get back.

Healing is needed
Strength and peace, as well
The world, I mean the devil is a lie
I once was under its spell.

Shield don't fail me now
Confess and make amends
God, what must I do to retract

Lose more friends or maybe sins?

I hate my decisions
But more I hate the outcome
I despise the uncertainty
What is life without one?

One love, one family
One God, one forever kiss
One way to make it right
One prayer and it's for this.

I pray that her heart and mine
Will be forever intertwined
No matter the place or time
No matter where I search I will find.

Us, under the same roof
The same bed, the same loop
The same ideology of life
The same passion, the same roots.

I will always keep the faith
Work on me and become better
But God, if You can help a brother out
This will be my last letter.

The words are flowing rapidly
Truth is whole not a piece
And the fact is I feel more calm now
Sometimes you just have to release.

André Sneed

HARD LESSON LEARNED

I had a talk with God today
Realizing that I really lost my way
I didn't recognize the mirror
'Who did I think I am,' I'd say.

Full of my own intention
Falling victim of proverbs twenty-one two
I cried a river full of remorse
Submitted to the altar in my living room.

I've been ignoring the signs
God warned me along the way
He sent me several messages
But prideful ignorance led to disarray.

The suppression of truth
Trapped in the pool of self-medicating
Attempting to bury a version of me
A doppelganger emerged for relating.

How did I get here?
How could I allow it to be?
Maybe a better question is
What would be said from a wiser me?

He would say, Come back to God
Stop seeking your own understanding
Follow the divine light
The foundation of Christ is for the standing.

Dive deep in your word, rebuild
Pray regularly with your spouse

Your Perspective is Not My Reality

Place God at the head to lead you
Proclaim His praises from your mouth.

I am Aligned now and realize my err
Selfish in my ways without a care
Unwilling to recognize who I'd become
Apologies to all; I am released from stun.

I listened but didn't hear
Halfway living my true life
One foot in reality and one in the past
Just as days turn to night.

I must grow with the times
Old lifestyles must be disavowed
No dwelling on familiar habits
Unless I am envisioning God's child.

And to the matters of concernment
I must focus on respect and the process
This time is for healing
No more will I run off my own logic.

I pray daily and fluently
I study on a schedule these days
I will never return to the other guy
I'm determined to be stuck in His ways.

I have repented and vowed to change
Prayer for forgiveness, confirmed
He tore me down to build me up
Call it a hard lesson learned.

André Sneed

SIMPLY NOTORIOUS

Lately, secretly I've been crying
There is no need for me lying
My insides are rapidly dying
Let me free my feelings from hiding.

I'm tired of the sadness
I'm bottled with emotional consume
The release is necessary
Periodically, I presume.

The walls of my room
Confide in my intentions
And if walls could talk
I recommend you not listen.

It is my mission
To protect from the messy
But, if I spew lessons
Grade yourself and don't test me.

I'm far from stable
But, does my actions look it?
I'm tripping in my mind
And wondering who booked it.

A nonstop flight and my neck has a crick in it
Why are my folk overlooking it
Who grabbed my heart, shook it
My notifications are missing a push in it.

Is it because we all have bags
I'm checking a minimum of three
How can the world keep its turns

While I'm running on empty?

If you hate me, just miss me
Walk on by, don't tempt me
I don't lose, so I must humor me
No exception to the rule of three.

I close my eyes but I see
Cut the tip of my thumb but feel me
Lost my smell and taste, but I still eat
So hear me when I say I'm still G.

My senses stay keen
But I seem to have a dirty spleen
That's definition one and two
Take it how you want it, thief's theme.

This is my reassurance
No one else can endure this
This war was built for me
A warrior with a boxer's endurance.

If you're in my life you're a tourist
On the bull, cause I'm a Taurus
In the heat of a moment
Remembering the times being victorious.

Doesn't it feel glorious
Borderline luxurious
I'm different, But still free
With a part of me that's simply notorious.

André Sneed

2020 VISION

2020's vision is about karma and truth
2020's vision is exactly what it seems
God's revelation of the err in our ways
The worst and the best, like a crazy dream.

2020's vision is extreme, and all-knowing
Look at 2020's vision and see what it's showing
We have lost our way and selfish to others
Remember family, giving, and forgiveness to brothers.

My vision is 2016 which is optically better
If my 2016 vision could have written me a letter
It probably would say, keep a 2010 mind state
God first, family next, then a clean slate.

Yet, 2020's vision does not see it being too late
2020 is about change at an enormous rate
God, please order are steps and move us forward
Align us with your will as we come toward.

The gates of heaven, through a life fulfilled
This rabbit hole is so deep it gives me chills
But (the greatest conjunction in the word)
But God, will bring us through with no deserve.

I pray for healing, understanding, peace
Strength, serenity, revelation, tranquility
Wisdom, growth, and community
For the world, my family, friends, and me.

Promise to change and follow through
Continue to love and spread love too

Do it today, right now, reconnaissance view
Refuse to let the enemy hold power over you.

God's love is undying, omnipotent, omnipresent
Unwavering, unchanging, overzealous
Agape, He is in you, take heed and listen
Find your way, your route, in His 2020 vision.

André Sneed

BEAUTIFULLY BROKEN

Sometimes God has to break us
In a few pieces like a platter
But sometimes we need remolding
So our pieces must be shattered.

Caught in this life of ownership
My wife, my kids, my whip, my lid
My house, my shoes, my ways
My grind, everything but what I did.

Listen hear you dig, follow the lights
They lead to something
That's what my inner god said
There's a reason you're here with nothing.

Broken to molecules after combust
So I did away with the lust
Honestly, I did away with much
Now, I'd rather give it away it's a must.

I'd rather help others as a primary
Whenever I think of myself, stop
Give again and kick knowledge
Like a 90s OG on the block.

No monkeys on my watch
There's no time for foolishness
I once found myself in a room of "kings"
Asking, whose royal fool is this?

Had to change my palace
And thoughts deemed the screwiest
Aligned my heart and actions

But give me time, I admit I am new at this.

André Sneed

BOOT CAMP

God is with me, I'm not alone
But it feels sad being one in this home
I've become better
But now I am ready to become whole.

God complete me, then completely
Bind my soul with my true love
I'm not searching whereabouts
My soul mate ordained from above.

I've seen both sides
Now I'm ready to face it all
I'm not afraid of anything usually
Not to try, fail, or even fall.

But seclusion in the midst of the plan
I look at my peers, and man
There are a lot of people hurting
What makes me better or a different man?

I can only feel that I deserve
How blissful of me
My equal is not present
That's the past vision I'd see.

But I wanted to be better
Now I want to be the best
I'm waiting for a reciprocal reward
But must be patient in this flesh.

Blessed, still, I cannot deny this
I work for everything, I never wished

Some things cannot be obtained through work
Somethings are given, not of this earth.

I've stayed away from lying
And that's even to myself
But somehow I've reverted to crying
Concerned about my mental health.

But God said my debt has been paid
And to rely on my faith and be brave
Positive vibes only, ride the wave
Living in my truth, militate change.

André Sneed

ELLIPSIS

Life is in the dots in between the years
From life to death, isn't it clear?
This world is what you make it
Who you reach is in your grasp, take it.

God first, family next, then off to the races
Striving for completion minus complacent
Help your brother Bro, watch over sis
Goals of needs and wants, but not wish.

Talents are God's personal blessings
He uses you to help others
Random acts of kindness
Prepare to do His work and bless another.

Push, rest some and press harder
The sloth inside us has God bothered
Malice in our heart will never be a friend
Forgiveness will free you not revenge.

Use fear as fuel, and pain as strength
Keep your intentions pure and mint
Giving up, not an option today
Geographic's are just a place to stay.

Live right now, impede on the enemy's plan
Do your best with a smile, you're a man
Accomplish great things, give God praise
Embrace your joy; it never fades.

Things are just things, Love is everlasting
Words are powerful, but more is action

Basting in Agape with levels deep as the sea
Make sure your ellipsis breeds legacy.

André Sneed

FACE THE MUSIC

Too old to be repeating these patterns
Already learned that lesson before
So now it's more about ridding bad habits
And stacking good ones, sky to floor.

I have tasted that for sure
Smell it, I smelled it before
Seen it a thousand times
Heard it when it evolved and origin pure.

Finally came to my senses
So now I have to stick with it
Don't think I'm better than others
Just exploring my potential, I finally did it.

All good things happen in time
But, I see the flaws in mine
It's hard to watch the reruns in my mind
I could have been shined.

No worries, now is the time
Let's keep sight on the direction
Replace unneeded then entrepreneur grind
And pray for urges to lessen.

Watch yourself grow
Baste a little in the glow
After all, you will earn it
Now thank God and let it go.

And now you want more
It feels good past the surface

Did a hundred and ten on my wants
Doing a buck fifty on my purpose.

I know it makes them nervous,
Who would have ever thought
That they would have even heard this
Besides the wise patiently waiting for my service.

Thanks
I know everyone's drum pattern is different
But my wave fully matches my vibe
This tune is more than just a listen.

A Humble classic in disguise
But, expect faces to deny your verb
Still step out on faith, lay the verse
And let the joyous sound be heard.

Internally first,
Then throughout the land
Breed healthy competition with self
Then blaze a trail for the next man.

André Sneed

LET'S GET ON WITH IT

From deep in the darkness
I can see the Leer
Based on the shadows
But I see it clear.

A tingle on my neck
When it draws near
I'm feeling emotions
But refuse to drop a tear.

Smelling my pheromones
You won't recognize fear
I know that you're evil
I can identify peer.

Driving me crazy
When I lost steer
On task with purpose
His reason I'm here.

No more running in circles
Gasping for air
A brand new circle of life
No need for a spare.

I'm pulling my load
No longer my hair
My social is anti
Feeling no need for a share.

Friends and family
Right now seems rare

So in my world
Remains without care.

And only apparel
I consider being pair
Reality will bite
It's hard but fair.

Life is a trip
I'm facetious while I'm there
But when I'm back in my niche
Returns the thinking stare.

I'm ready for war
When I leave my lair
With my armor of God
Deploy if you dare.

André Sneed

THANKS IN ADVANCE

What if I knew
I would be an author who is published
On the local news twice
Spreading positivity to the public.

What if I knew
I would be a college grad
Reaching every goal I set
Thanks to the push from my Dad.

What if I knew
My personalized works, right now
Would be on the peoples walls
Or I would write lovers' vows.

What if I knew
I'd never have more than I can handle
Like parenthood and marriage
Growing fond of international travel.

What if I knew
My dreams would come to fruition
The business goals I aspired
Fell in line with my vision.

What if I knew
My voice is more than words on a line
Being capable to touch a life
Like being the best man five times.

What if I knew
Through it all, what I considered a win
Is being happy within yourself

Peace glowing your own shiny skin.

What if I knew
The beauty of being Grand
A love for your kids' children
Not even they can understand.

What if I knew
Purpose aligned with will
Breeds greatness undeserved
Yet, a destiny fulfilled.

What if I knew
My purpose is more like a stance
I would greet my loving God
And say 'thanks in advance!'

André Sneed

THE LONE PALINDROME

I have to stop filling the void
With material things, they're not you
Do I really need another pair of shoes
All the jewelry does not seem to soothe.

Designer clothes, tell me what's the use
I feel like I'm the one that's being used
Trying to solve a puzzle minus a clue
Ouch, watch out; here comes the truth.

Only I can make myself happy
But what is the blueprint to success?
I'm feeling my best, looking my best
But part of my heart is cold, I attest.

Not looking for love; this is partly due
No one can fill that glass slipper shoe
I'm a better me, but she is not you
Not her, or her, what is a man to do?

I'm looking for placement or is it sanction
I just want what I'm truly deserved
Wait, do I have it now, no
This is not promised, from the God I serve.

I got some nerve, that's part of the problem
This equation is tough I need solving
Confidence plus stubbornness equates
To a love deficit and material solvents.

No matter the addition, a loss in my eyes
My math always results in the great divide
Emptiness looks like an empty nest home

In one word, deified led to my palindrome.

André Sneed

WHAT WILL IT BE

You're searching for a future in love
Kind, secure, and free
I've found I'm more content
In these moments presently.

Being in love with my creator
Is much more heavenly
Plus, my issue with trust is
It no longer lies with me.

And you can lie to yourself
I'm focused on my inner Chi
No late applications
Rejecting negative energy.

And what comes next
Is you think I'm acting selfishly
But it's God, family, then me
I'd say that's standard, don't you agree?

Another time and head space
It might be something I can see
But a remolding of my heart
Is happening currently.

From the gate of the race
We knew this was temporarily
And you've never run a marathon
So let's just enjoy this spree.

Is it personal, no
Bad timing, yes, indeed

But we always have an option
So tell me, what will it be?

André Sneed

THE PLACEHOLDER

You want me to hold you down
I just want to raise you up
But, that's not what you're looking for
So, let me be the one to say enough.

I'm no longer searching for love
Let's have fun in the moments and times
You see yellow and smash the gas
I see yield and won't ignore the signs.

This time, I'm, going to be the realest
To myself, all of the time
So manifestations of friendships shine
But, when coins drop of the smallest size.

Be ready, stay steady, protect you
Your feelings and your emotions
Consistent with my actions & words
Can't say I led you on or had you open.

Not into wishing and hoping
Stray away from sadness and moping
Don't gauge your worth with token
Your weaknesses and insecurities are eloping.

When did you say you're going to quit smoking?
You must be really joking
I see infatuation in the eyes of thee
Two months, two weeks, you don't know me.

I'm getting money, then the gym
You're skipping work for the D
Right now, I'm researching a Roth IRA

I can call you when I'm free.

No more settling for me
No need for perfection to be
But, self-betterment, a clean temple, yes
No drama, no clinging, no negativity.

Tell me how we can be
Our goals don't align, and that's fine
But sex is cardio or a state of mind
And you can never be mine.

I don't want to waste your time
You act like you're moving in
Trying to redefine the term of friend
We have two different definitions of win.

See, I'm trying to curb the sin
You are just trying to fit in
Something like the placeholder
Between my start and your end.

André Sneed

PICK A SIDE

Forgive but won't forget
I'm not done yet
Betray me, stab my back
I won't wait for what's next.

Wearing a Teflon mental vest
Kevlar on my chest
We all hate being played
Attention: this is not a test.

Went straight to the left
Your heart is a mess
So evil, disloyal at best
Couldn't have seen it if I guessed.

Not a family crest
More like a gathering of pests
I'm glad my kids are grown
I'm definitely emptying the nest.

No need to confess
I see it in between the text
But you crossed all the lines
I seek solitude and rest.

Awake now, too much I slept
They really came for my death
Talking amongst themselves
Until dark secrets were fetched.

The only way I can stay true
Stop shopping the brand new

Focusing on my next moves
So, see you when I see you.

And for you and the others
Who feel slightly torn inside
Next time you should decide
Man up and pick a side.

André Sneed

SUPREME ANIMAL

When you find out you're in a game
You didn't know that she was dealing
And your cards are not the same
You're pitching friends, she's catching feelings.

This halts the process of healing
But she resents me pulling back
Then you realize you're in a play
And she doesn't know how to act.

This new scene is obscene
The dramas getting deep as an ocean
But with subtle waves most days
Passive-aggressive displays of emotion.

Like the role of a parent
Have control don't let yours run hectic
I cannot be mad at your nature
So don't be mad at my perspective.

Now you understand this is learning
You don't have to like my ideology
But dropping out is not concerning
And one's happiness resides in thee.

So don't try and cage an animal free
First lesson of the elective
Conduct yourself with class, or not
Just respect my perspective.

But if you decide to test this
A killjoy will find herself a chew toy

And a real student enjoys the truth
Turn your Pinocchio to a good boy.

My life is my life
Like a personal movie reel
And even though you're in the picture
I can make this video a still.

Making your now an until
Dragged by an opposition of will
This beast ripping out of my arm
Is not just cast, he's top bill.

From the beginning, I kept it real
Somehow my words twist in your mind
I told you I was different
And my actions show I'm one of a kind.

But you confused a my for mine
I'm going to say this one last time
If we agree to be friends, we're friends
Or it's curtains call, fin, end of lines.

André Sneed

MISS ELOQUENT

She captured a space in my mind
Her gaze amazed; it was one of a kind
Honestly, it gave me a tingled spine
Her sapiosexuality depicted a mime.

A gift for the taking, let's call her mine
In love with how my ideas leave a shine
How words weave together and bind
Poetic to the ear, like music note lines.

Like beauty seen solely in the eyes
A game of three truths minus the lies
Like a walk, imitating a slow grind
Equipped with bowed legs & gapped thighs.

Her spirit and energy, I felt like the blind
So no matter what, we had a great time
I was roped into the fineness of her wine
As if her wildflower produced grape vine.

Beautifully flawed, her heart and mind
Even from the front, I sight her behind
She came with envy and left me a lime
If you were to rate her, call her a dime.

Because of whom she is on the inside
With the wit to match, a slippery slide
And a cute smile with a mysterious side
So hold the death, she's down to ride.

A little mischievous, to my surprise
Thinking of the ways our soul will be tied

Your Perspective is Not My Reality

What do you expect when nature rise?
More than a beat, this Miss is a vibe.

Whether pretty and fierce or subtle and shy
Bold and outgoing or chill and fly
Even Johnny would say, my my my
This Miss is eloquent, so kneel and abide.

André Sneed

INFINITE MUSE

Fate breeding origins of life
Relating through familiarity and pain
Friendship is the root of the journey
Let's say Love, to give it a name.

Soulmates, divine, undying love
Yin & Yang, a pairing from above
Sometimes we stall, needing a nudge
Memories of you are a consuming mental flood.

The elevation of your thoughts
The passion behind your intentions
The gentleness of your spirit
And your physique, I'd like to mention.

The beauty in your eyes
A smile radiating heat so warm
Demeanor of everything right in the world
No prerequisite of adorn.

I adore you, genuinely is the key
The family we've become
Growing up from kids to raising kids
Don't close the book, we're not done.

I will always love you for destiny is true
A lifetime of forever or maybe two
I will die before I fail, in rightly loving you
My queen, my goddess, my infinite muse.

STAY

Last night I watched you sleep
I never seen a better sense of peace
A daily ritual release
Beauty, securely wrapped in a sheet.

I wanted to rise and take flee
But wouldn't take chance of thee
Waking you out of the deep
REM, so I remained and stayed neat.

Messy is the selfish
Thinking only of ones self-need
But I know your super powers
I really, should have washed your feet.

That sounds Godly to me
Rest here on the couch comfortably
I thought of embracing your temple
But chose to gaze in awe humbly.

Much of nothing to do with me
But, tell me how this could be
God blessed me with a friendship
Spanning over a quarter century?

It sounds like the opposite of grief
Let's call it joy, confidently
Never once bit our tongues
And always respect each other's speech.

Would never let another badly speak
Love each other's valleys and peaks

André Sneed

Even if time would lapse
Our rhythm never skipped a beat.

Music moving hearts and feet
Still fusing lyrics and harmony
Brown Sugar, you ready to eat
But no eggs and no bologna.

This is home with my homie
Not out there roaming
And genuine love is a high
Minus the pains of growing.

True, some things are better
And some are best not knowing
As much as I want to make my way
I find myself not going.

PILLOW TALK

I miss spoiling my miss
Conversations after bliss
Trading aspirations as we lay
Saying 'we should do this.'

Let's go to a museum
And share interpretations
Watch the sun rise on a beach
After staring at constellations.

Take a walk in nature
Get back to soulful love
Reveal our inner truths
Give gifts just because.

The world is our oyster
And I'm dying of thirst
So won't you be my water
As I place your needs first.

Look at your beautiful skin
How your curves blend in
Your eyes drown my gaze
Will this feeling ever end?

Like a perpetual whirlwind
With no corners to bend
Let's freeway ride in the wind
Stream Jill over and again.

Follow rose petals pathways
Made for precious feet to walk

André Sneed

Leading to a heart-shaped bath
For our love to get lost.

Like that moment in the film
When the song sets a tone
You get that tingly sensation
And cry, smile, or moan.

Hear the horns blown
The symphonies going strong
The cords finesse its own
This is the life I call home.

I dream of falling in love
Better yet to stand in it
A beauty with no spoils
Perfection embracing blemish.

SILVER LAKE

With him, her comfort level
Was way higher than a little
It's been so long, yet the first time
Her shyness made her giggle.

Fitting together like a puzzle
Making way past the riddle
Sharing so much over the years
Except for the pieces in the middle.

Kisses were softer than a pillow
Beautiful bodies like willows
Orange polish glowing in the dark
She enjoyed Kelly's tempo.

Taking my time tonight
Complexity reaching past simple
Wetting her canvas with my brush
And forming groove with my chisel.

Foreplay to the instrumental
Finally made it past our mental
Since we were out of our heads
We decided to share vittles.

With a taste so fresh
Exciting our palate, no dental
This feels so sweet, tender and nostalgic
Let's call it sentimental.

A night of passion so gentle
Blue aura shining on my dimples

André Sneed

Over a quarter century in the making
A silver lake with moon gazed ripples.

GENTLEMAN WILD

Are you looking for a gentleman
Or a wild boy, wait, why choose
What I Consistently offer are both
You don't have to lose.

Unpredictable yet dependable
Governing the waves of sin
Perfect balance, benevolence
Against the malice within.

Freak in the bed, hood in the street
Cool nerd for conversation
Slick with the hustle and grind
A gentleman for relations.

God first, family next
Then I'm all about the dough
Treat you like a queen
Yet pull your hair and give a choke.

Slapping your backside
Makes my nature rise
Envisioning my entire head
Deep in between those thighs.

Pleasure first, for you
Trust me miss I'm a giver
And I'm so ready to eat
I know I just ate dinner.

No take out, yes I deliver
No finesse, I confess I'm engorged

André Sneed

And I won't enter until you shiver
Is this more than you bargained for?

I don't play, I'm not a kid
But let me be your toy
Let's be impulsive and spontaneous
Adrenaline produces great joy.

Still I handle my business
I got the bills and funds on lock
And I love when a plan comes together
It all makes my heartbeat knock.

This is just an overview
If you are with it, let's make some noise
If it's something rich or even quick
You'll find it in a gentleman & wild boy.

THE ID

I want you
Lips, kiss, touch, and stride
Walk for me baby
And watch my nature rise.

Finger tips on your body
Hand around your neck
Sharing my energy
Leading to subtle gropes of your chest.

Your body feels my breath
Inhaling with anticipation
Licking your torso
Gently peeling back your casing.

Provisions for the tasting
No time will I be wasting
Experience the bliss
Act II is forceful penetration.

Slow long strokes
Followed by hard quick thrusts
Lick your breasts
And follow by stirring it up.

Turn over
I want it from the back
Grab your cheeks
Spread them wide, and attack.

Now on your side
Put that ankle on my shoulder

André Sneed

I got the nerve, watch the curve
I'm starting to get bolder.

I bit your lip
Hand back on your neck
Wait, where are you going
I'm not done yet.

Brown eye in my vision
I beat it to submission
The neighbors know my adjectives
Every time they listen.

Far from defeat
But the climax took a seat
Love or judge, but respect
The carnal Id in me.

REPLAY

As I lay in this bed that just was a sled
Reminiscing on a taste, feeling well fed
My mind is in a loop, that's all I know
Just like the track, Living Room Flow.

Gifted extra sauce, my late night treat
How did she know, the days I cheat
With sweets, my chocolate delight
Her neck looked inviting; I took a bite.

Ecstasy, is getting the best of me
The only thing missing is her next to me
Kisses from her lips, as soft as pillows
Whispering words without the riddles.

She kept calling him the rock
We fit together like key and lock
Her spout was wide open dripping wet
The second scene started with a mess.

I upped the pace she tightened her embrace
Followed by the uncontrollable leg shake
No, it's not a race, it's a pleasure marathon
If this was still summer, it would be dawn.

What a ride, she never asked me to stop
She just used her hand, to block her spot
I took it for a sign she wanted a choke
No matter what, I never stopped the stroke.

I've never seen a masterpiece, so petite
Like a narrow lane on a curvy street

André Sneed

I held my release, I didn't want it to cease
Until she told me to let it off the leash.

You would think it stopped right there
But tell that to my lustful smirk and stare
Memories bound to my mental stay
With audio on repeat and visions on replay.

LOVE @ RANDOM

Anticipating synergy from a wildflower
A partner in the wild to hunt & devour
Standing in love and all the above
Trust and believe this world is ours.

I'm just a green-eyed Black Panther
In search of a shiny coat cougar
Shapely, with a cute laugh & smile
And a walk that says, look at me now.

I'll love her random outbursts
Loud off tune singing a verse
Impromptu urges of activities
A mutual respect for proclivities.

I mean her propensity gives rise
To my nature, emotion, and my eyes
Never having to hide or disguise
Expecting the unexpected is advised.

Someone who will want to stay up late
Stare into my eyes as we conversate
Let's do a dinner and movie date
Bring an overnight bag it's in another state.

She'll be bright and seen like a star
Yet, down to earth by far
She'll keep to herself and stay up to par
But always ready to love scene in a car.

Loving to keep many coins in the jar
When opportunity arrives, the door is ajar

André Sneed

Providing a word when in need of a bar
Giving me space, she can see from Mars.

She expects respect and not to phantom
Just a free spirit who thinks I'm handsome
She is always down to ride; call her tandem
By now you get it, this is a love at random.

ABOUT THE AUTHOR

Poetry artist André Sneed is a lover of words. A free- spirited individual with the ideology that all emotion, logic, spirituality, creativity, and real-life situations can be displayed with elegance.

There is no extreme he will not explore or any message he is timid to convey for the benefit of being genuine for the reader. Life is an adventure, and he believes every day is an opportunity to live, teach, laugh, share, and more importantly, strive.

www.ingramcontent.com/pod-product-compliance
Lightning Source LLC
Chambersburg PA
CBHW051233120626
46547CB00013B/1618